Adventures
in Japanese 1

Hiragana and *Katakana* Workbook

アドベンチャー
日本語 1

ひらがな ＆ カタカナ
ワークブック

Adventures in Japanese 1

Hiragana & Katakana Workbook

Hiromi Peterson

Illustrated by Michael Muronaka & Emiko Kaylor

Cheng & Tsui Company

17 16 15 14 13 12 11 10 09   5 6 7 8 9 10

First edition 1998
2009 Printing

Cheng & Tsui Company, Inc.
25 West Street
Boston, MA 02111-1213 USA
www.cheng-tsui.com
"Bringing Asia to the World"™

Hiragana and *Katakana* Workbook
ISBN 978-0-88727-302-5

Textbooks, companion workbooks, and audio recordings are also available from the publisher.

Printed in Canada

ADVENTURES IN JAPANESE 1
HIRAGANA & KATAKANA WORKBOOK

CONTENTS

ひらがな

Start from the right column. s = stop, t = tail, h = hook.　　　　　　　　　↓

O	E	*U	I	A
お	え	う	い	あ
お	え	う	い	あ
お	え	う	い	あ

* う is used in writing the second O in the long vowel sound OO. Ex. どうぞ DOOZO, さようなら SAYOONARA. However, there are some exceptions which you must learn as they are introduced.

1

ひらがな

アドベンチャー日本語1

ひらがな 1-2 （あ～お）　　　　なまえ NAMAE (Name): _____

【 よみましょう : Let's read.】

1.	い	stomach	6.	あお	blue (color)
2.	え	painting	7.	おい	nephew
3.	お	tail	8.	うえ	up, above
4.	あい	love	9.	ええ	yes
5.	いえ	house	10.	いいえ	no

【 ✎ かきましょう : Let's write.】

I. Write A, I, U, E, O horizontally and vertically five times each without looking at the chart.

A. horizontally

B. vertically

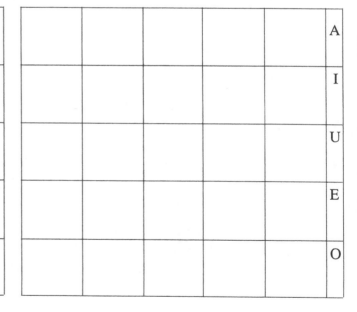

II. Write the words in *hiragana*.

1. Yes (Informal)　　_____ _____
　　　　　　　　　　　　e　　　　e

2. No　　　　　　　_____ _____ _____
　　　　　　　　　　i　　　　i　　　　e

ひらがな　　　　　　　　　　2

Start from the right column. s = stop, t = tail, h = hook.　　　　　　↓

KO	KE	KU	KI	KA
こ	け	く	き	か
こ	け	く	き	か
こ	け	く	き	か

ひらがな

Start from the right column. s = stop, t = tail, h = hook.   ↓

GO	GE	GU	GI	GA
ご	け	ぐ	ぎ	が
ご	げ	ぐ	ぎ	が
ご	げ	ぐ	ぎ	が

ひらがな 2 - 3 （あ～ご）　　　　　　　　なまえ NAMAE : _____

【 よみましょう : Let's read.】

1.	あき	autumn, fall	6.	かお	face
2.	かい	seashell	7.	かぎ	key
3.	いけ	pond	8.	かげ	shadow
4.	こい	carp	9.	けいこ	Keiko (Japanese girl's name)
5.	きかい	machine	10.	あきお	Akio (Japanese boy's name)

【 かきましょう : Let's write.】

I. Write A, I, U, E, O, KA, KI, KU, KE, KO, GA, GI, GU, GE, GO vertically THREE times each without looking at the chart.

G	K		
			A
			I
			U
			E
			O

G	K		
			A
			I
			U
			E
			O

G	K		
			A
			I
			U
			E
			O

II. Write these names in *hiragana*.

1. Aoki (Family) _____ _____ _____　　　　4. Keiko (Female's) _____ _____ _____

2. Ueki (Family) _____ _____ _____　　　　5. Kikuko (Female's) _____ _____ _____

3. Akagi (Family) _____ _____ _____　　　　6. Akio (Male's) _____ _____ _____

ひらがな

ORIGINS OF HIRAGANA: PART 1

All of the symbols of the *hiragana* are derived originally from Chinese characters. Here are the original Chinese characters from which each *hiragana* developed and their three different styles of penmanship. In each group, the first column on the left shows the modern *kana* symbol; the second column shows the *kanji* from which that *kana* was derived, with the *kanji* written in KAISHO style (regular style); the third column shows the same *kanji* in GYOOSHO style (walking style); and the fourth column shows the *kanji* in SOOSHO style (grass style).

	Hiragana	Kaisho	Gyoosho	Soosho		Hiragana	Kaisho	Gyoosho	Soosho
A	あ	安	安	あ	KA	か	加	加	か
I	い	以	以	い	KI	き	幾	幾	き
U	う	宇	宇	う	KU	く	久	久	く
E	え	衣	衣	え	KE	け	計	計	け
O	お	於	於	お	KO	こ	己	己	こ

アドベンチャー日本語1   なまえ NAMAE (Name)   : _____

ひらがな 3 - 1   ひづけ HIZUKE (Date)   : _____

Start from the right column. s = stop, t = tail, h = hook.   ↓

SO	SE	SU	SHI	SA
そ	せ	す	し	さ
そ	せ	す	し	さ
そ	せ	す	し	さ

ひらがな

Start from the right column. s = stop, t = tail, h = hook.　　　　　　　　　↓

ZO		ZE		ZU		JI		ZA	
	ぞ		ぜ		ず		じ		ざ
	ぞ		ぜ		ず		じ		ざ

ひらがな3-3　（あ〜ぞ）　　　なまえ NAMAE (Name): _____

【 😊 よみましょう : Let's read.】

1. おすし　　　sushi (polite)　　　　6. うし　　　cow

2. おかし　　　sweets; candy　　　　7. かぜ　　　a cold

3. せかい　　　world　　　　　　　　8. おじ　　　uncle

4. ござ　　　　beach mat　　　　　　9. すき　　　like

5. ぞう　　　　elephant　　　　　　10. おさけ　　rice wine (polite)

【 ✎ かきましょう : Let's write.】

I. Write A, I, U, E, O, KA, KI, KU, KE, KO, GA, GI, GU, GE, GO, SA, SHI, SU, SE, SO, ZA, JI, ZU, ZE, ZO vertically TWO times each without looking at the chart.

Z	S	G	K		
					A
					I
					U
					E
					O

Z	S	G	K		
					A
					I
					U
					E
					O

II. Write the words in *hiragana*.

1. Seki (Family name) _____ _____　　　6. sushi _____ _____

2. Suzuki (Family name) _____ _____ _____　　　7. sake (rice wine) _____ _____

3. Seiko (Female's name) _____ _____ _____　　　8. Saeko (Female's) _____ _____ _____

4. Aosaka (Family name _____ _____ _____ _____　　　9. four [shi] _____

5. Asakusa (town name) _____ _____ _____ _____　　　10. five [go] _____

9

ひらがな

ORIGINS OF HIRAGANA: PART 2

In each group, the first column on the left shows the modern *kana* symbol; the second column shows the *kanji* from which that *kana* was derived, with the *kanji* written in KAISHO style (regular style); the third column shows the same *kanji* in GYOOSHO style (walking style); and the fourth column shows the *kanji* in SOOSHO style (grass style).

	Hiragana	Kaisho	Gyoosho	Soosho
SA	さ	左	さ	さ
SHI	し	え	え	し
SU	す	す	す	す
SE	せ	世	せ	せ
SO	そ	曽	曽	そ

	Hiragana	Kaisho	Gyoosho	Soosho
TA	た	太	た	た
CHI	ち	知	知	ち
TSU	つ	川	り	つ
TE	て	天	て	て
TO	と	止	止	と

Start from the right column. s = stop, t = tail, h = hook.　　　　　　　　　　↓

TO	TE	TSU	CHI	TA

ひらがな

Start from the right column. s = stop, t = tail, h = hook.　　　　　　　　↓

DO		DE		ZU *2		JI *1		DA	
ど		で		づ		ぢ		だ	
	ど		で		づ		ぢ		だ
	ど		で		づ		ぢ		だ

*1　ぢ is used only for words relating to the word "blood" (ち).

*2　づ is used following another つ or for a ZU sound which is derived from a word originally
　　written with a つ.

アドベンチャー日本語1

ひらがな４-３ （あ〜ど） なまえ NAMAE (Name): _____

【 よみましょう : Let's read.】

1. て　　　　　hand
2. と　　　　　door
3. ちず　　　　map
4. つき　　　　moon
5. てつお　　　(Male's name)

6. おだ　　　　(Family name)
7. つだ　　　　(Family name)
8. たけした　　(Family name)
9. あきた　　　(Family name)
10. たかだ　　　(Family name)

【 かきましょう : Let's write.】

I. Fill in the blanks with the correct hiragana. Use う for the second O sound in a word with the long vowel OO.

1. _____ _____ _____ _____ _____ ね _____ 。 (It's hot!)
　　 A　　 tsu　　 i　　 de　　 su　 ne　 e.

_____ _____ _____ _____ ね _____ 。 (Yes, it is!)
　 So　　 o　　 de　　 su　 ne　 e.

2. _____ _____ ん _____ _____ _____ _____ 。 (How are you?)
　　 O　　 ge　 n　 ki　 de　 su　 ka

は _____ 、 _____ ん _____ _____ _____ 。 (Yes, I am fine.)
Ha　 i　　　　 ge　 n　 ki　 de　 su

3. _____ _____ も _____ り _____ _____ _____ (Thank you very much.)
　 Do　 o　 mo　 a　 ri　 ga　 to　 o

_____ _____ _____ ま _____ 。 (Thank you very much.)
　 go　 za　 i　 ma　 su

_____ _____ _____ _____ _____ ま _____ _____ 。 (You are welcome.)
　 Do　 o　 i　 ta　 shi　 ma　 shi　 te

4. は _____ め ま _____ _____ 。 (How do you do?)
　 Ha　 ji　 me ma　 shi　 te

わ _____ _____ は _____ _____ _____ _____ _____ 。 (I am Aoki.)
Wa　 ta　 shi　 wa　 A　 o　 ki　 de　 su

_____ _____ _____ よ ろ _____ _____ 。 (Nice to meet you.)
　 Do　 o　 zo　 yo ro　 shi　 ku

13

ひらがな

ORIGINS OF HIRAGANA: PART 3

In each group, the first column on the left shows the modern *kana* symbol; the second column shows the *kanji* from which that *kana* was derived, with the *kanji* written in KAISHO style (regular style); the third column shows the same *kanji* in GYOOSHO style (walking style); and the fourth column shows the *kanji* in SOOSHO style (grass style).

	Hiragana	Kaisho	Gyoosho	Soosho		Hiragana	Kaisho	Gyoosho	Soosho
NA	な	奈	奈	な	HA	は	波	波	は
NI	に	仁	仁	に	HI	ひ	比	比	ひ
NU	ぬ	奴	奴	ぬ	HU	ふ	不	不	ふ
NE	ね	祢	祢	ね	HE	へ	部	部	へ
NO	の	乃	乃	の	HO	ほ	保	保	ほ

Start from the right column. s = stop, t = tail, h = hook.　　　　　　　　　　↓

NO	NE	NU	NI	NA
の	ね	ぬ	に	な
の	ね	ぬ	に	な
の	ね	ぬ	に	な

【 よみましょう : Let's read.】

1.	あなた	you	6.	うなぎ	eel
2.	ねこ	cat	7.	かに	crab
3.	なか	inside	8.	ねぎ	green onion
4.	いぬ	dog	9.	かたな	sword
5.	のど	throat	10.	のぐち	(Family name)

【 かきましょう : Let's write.】

I. Fill in the blanks with the correct hiragana. Use う for the second O sound of the long OO vowel.

1. ＿＿＿＿ れは ＿＿＿＿ ん ＿＿＿＿ ＿＿＿＿ ＿＿＿＿ 。 (What is that over there?)
　　　A　　re wa　　na　　n　　de　　su　　ka.

2. ＿＿＿ ＿＿＿ ＿＿＿ ＿＿＿ ＿＿＿ ＿＿＿ ＿＿＿ ＿＿＿ ＿＿＿ ＿＿＿ 。
　　Shi　　zu　　ka　　ni　　shi　　te　　ku　　da　　sa　　i.
　　(Please be quiet.)

3. ＿＿＿ ＿＿＿ ＿＿＿ ＿＿＿ ＿＿＿ ＿＿＿ ＿＿＿ ＿＿＿ 。 (It is cool!)
　　Su　　zu　　shi　　i　　　de　　su　　ne　　e.

4. Dog は 、 ＿＿＿ ほん ＿＿＿ ＿＿＿ 　 ＿＿＿ ん ＿＿＿
　　　　　　　wa　　　　ni　ho n　　go　　de　　　　na　　n　　to

　＿＿＿ ＿＿＿ ま ＿＿＿ ＿＿＿ 。　　(How do you say "dog" in Japanese?)
　　i　　i　　ma　　su　　ka.

5. ＿＿＿ ん ＿＿＿ ＿＿＿ は 。　　(Good afternoon.)
　　Ko　　n　　ni　　chi　　wa.

6. ＿＿＿ ＿＿＿ ＿＿＿ ＿＿＿ ＿＿＿ 。 (He is tardy.)
　　Chi　　ko　　ku　　de　　su.

7. ＿＿＿ ＿＿＿ ＿＿＿ (money)
　　O　　ka　　ne

8. ＿＿＿ よ ＿＿＿ ＿＿＿ ら 。 (Good-bye.)
　　Sa　　yo　　o　　na　　ra.

Start from the right column. s = stop, t = tail, h = hook.　　　　　　　　　　　↓

HO	HE *3	HU/FU *2	HI	HA *1
ほ	へ	ふ	ひ	は
ほ	へ	ふ	ひ	は
ほ	へ	ふ	ひ	は

*1　は is also pronounced WA when it is used as a topic particle.

*2　ふ is written as FU in ROOMAJI, but is pronounced like WHO. It is not pronounced as an English "f."

*3　へ is also pronounced E when it is used as a direction particle.

17　　　　　　　　　　　　　　　　　ひらがな

アドベンチャー日本語1　　　なまえ NAMAE (Name)　:＿＿＿＿＿＿＿＿＿＿＿＿＿

ひらがな６－２　　　　　　ひづけ HIZUKE (Date)　:＿＿＿＿＿＿＿＿＿＿＿＿＿

Start from the right column. s = stop, t = tail, h = hook.　　　　　↓

BO	BE	BU	BI	BA
ぼ	べ	ぶ	び	ば
	ぼ		べ		ぶ		び		ば
	ぼ		べ		ぶ		び		ば

Start from the right column.　s = stop, t = tail,　h = hook.　　　　　　　　　　↓

PO		PE		PU		PI		PA
ぽ		へ		ぷ		ぴ		ば
	ぽ		へ		ぷ		ぴ		ば
	ぽ		へ		ぷ		ぴ		ば

なまえ： _____

【 ✎ よみましょう : Let's read.】

1. は   tooth, teeth
2. ひと   person
3. へい   wall
4. ほし   star
5. おばけ   ghost

6. へび   snake
7. たび   travel
8. ぶどう   grape
9. かば   hippo
10. ばか   stupid, fool

【 ✎ かきましょう : Let's write.】

I. Fill in the blanks with the correct *hiragana*. Use は for the particle は. Use う for the second O of the long vowel OO.

1. _____ _____ _____ _____ _____ _____   _____ _____ _____ _____

   Ko   no   o   ka   ne   wa (particle)   a   na   ta   no

_____ _____ _____   (Is this money yours?)

   de   su   ka.

_____ _____ 、 _____ れ _____ わ _____ _____ _____ _____ _____

   Ha   i   so   re   wa (particle)   wa   ta   shi   no   de   su.

                     (Yes, that is mine.)

2. _____ _____ め ま _____ _____ 。   (How do you do?)

   Ha   ji   me   ma   shi   te.

_____ _____ _____ _____ _____ _____ _____ _____ 。 (I am Tanabe.)

   Bo   ku   wa (particle)   Ta   na   be   de   su.

_____ _____ _____ よ ろ _____ _____ 。 (Nice to meet you.)

   Do   o   zo   yo   ro   shi   ku.

3. _____ ん _____ _____ (pencil)

   e   n   pi   tsu

4. _____ _____ ん _____ (Japanese language)

   ni   ho   n   go

5. _____ _____ _____ (hat, cap)

   bo   o   shi

6. _____ や _____ 。 (Hurry up!)

   Ha   ya   ku.

8. _____ _____ よ _____ _____ _____ _____ ま _____ 。 (Good morning.)

   O   ha   yo   o   go   za   i   ma   su.

Start from the right column. s = stop, t = tail, h = hook.　　　　　　　　　↓

MO		ME		MU		MI		MA	
も		め		む		み		ま	
	も		め		む		み		ま
	も		め		む		み		ま

ひらがな

【 よみましょう：Let's read.】

1. め　　　　　eye
2. みず　　　　water
3. むし　　　　worm
4. なまえ　　　name
5. もしもし　　hello
6. むすび　　　rice ball
7. もち　　　　mochi
8. さしみ　　　raw fish
9. あめ　　　　rain; candy [different tone]
10. うめぼし　　pickled plum

【 ✎ かきましょう：Let's write.】

I. Fill in the blanks with the correct *hiragana*. Use う for the second O of the long vowel OO.

1. _____ _____ を _____ _____ _____ _____ _____ _____ _____ _____ 。
Ka　mi　o　i　chi　ma　i　ku　da　sa　i.
(Please give me one sheet of paper.)
_____ _____ 、_____ _____ _____ 。 (Here, please.)
Ha　i　do　o　zo.

2. _____ _____ を _____ _____ _____ _____ _____ _____ _____ 。
A　me　o　hi　to　tsu　ku　da　sa　i.
(Please give one piece of candy.)

3. _____ _____ を _____ _____ _____ _____ _____ _____ _____ 。
Ma　do　o　a　ke　te　ku　da　sa　i.
(Please open the window.)

_____ _____ _____ _____ _____ _____ _____ 。 (Please close it.)
Shi　me　te　ku　da　sa　i.

4. _____ _____ _____ _____ ん、_____ _____ _____ _____ ん 。
Su　mi　ma　se　n,　mi　e　ma　se　n.
(Sorry, I cannot see it.)

5. _____ _____ _____ _____ 。 (It is no good.)
Da　me　de　su.

6. _____ _____ _____ _____ _____ _____ _____ 。 (It is cold!)
Sa　mu　i　de　su　ne　e.

Start from the right column. s = stop, t = tail, h = hook.　　　　　　　　　　↓

YO			YU			YA

ひらがな

なまえ：＿＿＿＿＿＿＿＿＿＿＿＿＿＿＿＿

【 よみましょう : Let's read.】

1.　や　　　　　arrow
2.　おゆ　　　　hot water
3.　ゆき　　　　snow
4.　ゆうき　　　courage
5.　ゆめ　　　　dream

6.　ようこ　　　(Female's name)
7.　よしこ　　　(Female's name)
8.　やまだ　　　(Family name)
9.　やまもと　　(Family name)
10.　よしだ　　　(Family name)

【 かきましょう : Let's write.】

I. Fill in the blanks with the correct *hiragana*.

1. ＿＿＿ ＿＿＿ ＿＿＿ ＿＿＿ ＿＿＿ ＿＿＿ ＿＿＿ ＿＿＿ ＿＿＿ 。
　　O　　ha　　yo　　o　　go　　za　　i　　ma　　su.
　　　　　　　　　　　　　　　　　　　　　　　(Good morning.)

2. ＿＿＿ ＿＿＿ ＿＿＿ ＿＿＿ ん、＿＿＿ ＿＿＿ ＿＿＿ 。 (Yuko, hurry up.)
　　Yu　　u　　ko　　sa　　n　　ha　　ya　　ku.

3. ＿＿＿ ＿＿＿ ＿＿＿ ＿＿＿ ＿＿＿ ＿＿＿ 。　(He is absent.)
　　O　　ya　　su　　mi　　de　　su.

4. ＿＿＿ ＿＿＿ ＿＿＿ ＿＿＿ ＿＿＿ ＿＿＿ ＿＿＿ 。 (You did well.)
　　Yo　　ku　　de　　ki　　ma　　shi　　ta.

5. ＿＿＿ ん ＿＿＿ ＿＿＿ ＿＿＿ ＿＿＿ ＿＿＿ 。 (Please read.)
　　Yo　　n　de　　　ku　　da　　sa　　i.

6. ＿＿＿ ＿＿＿ を ＿＿＿ ＿＿＿ ＿＿＿ ＿＿＿ ＿＿＿ ＿＿＿ ＿＿＿ 。
　　A　　me　　o (particle)　fu　　ta　　tsu　　ku　　da　　sa　　i.
　　　　　　　　　　　　(Please give me two pieces of candies.)

7. ＿＿＿ ＿＿＿ ＿＿＿ ＿＿＿ ＿＿＿ ＿＿＿ 。 (Can you hear?)
　　Ki　　ko　　e　　ma　　su　　ka.

8. ＿＿＿ ＿＿＿ ＿＿＿ ＿＿＿ ＿＿＿ ＿＿＿ ＿＿＿ 。 (It is cold!)
　　Sa　　mu　　i　　de　　su　　ne　　e.

Start from the right column. s = stop, t = tail, h = hook.　　　　　　　　　　　　↓

RO	RE	RU	RI	RA
ろ	れ	る	り	ら
ろ	れ	る	り	ら
ろ	れ	る	り	ら

ひらがな

【 🙂 よみましょう : Let's read.】

1.	あり	ant	6.	よる	night
2.	いろ	color	7.	あられ	rice cracker
3.	りす	squirrel	8.	れきし	history
4.	しろ	castle	9.	こおり	ice
5.	はる	spring	10.	さむらい	samurai

【 ✎ かきましょう : Let's write.】

I. Fill in the blanks with the correct *hiragana*. Use は for the topic particle WA and う for lengthening the OO vowel.

1. _____ _____ _____ _____ _____ _____ _____ _____ _____
   Ha   ji   me   ma   shi   te   do   o   zo

   _____ _____ _____ _____ 。 (How do you do? Nice to meet you.)
   yo   ro   shi   ku.

2. _____ _____ _____ _____ _____ _____ _____ _____ _____ _____。
   Ko   re   wa (particle)   a   na   ta   no   de   su   ka.
               (Is this yours?)

3. ___ ___ ___ ___ ___ ___ ___ ___ ___ ___ ___ ___ ___。
   So   no   ke   shi   go   mu   wa (P)   bo   ku   no   de   su.
               (That eraser is mine.)

4. ___ ___ ___ ___ ___ ___ ___ ___ ___ ___ ___。
   A   ri   ga   to   o   go   za   i   ma   su.
               (Thank you very much.)

5. _____ _____ _____ _____ ん 。 (I do not know.)
   Shi   ri   ma   se   n.

6. ___ ___ を ___ ___ ___ ___ ___ ___ ___ ___。
   Ka   mi   o   i   chi   ma   i   ku   da   sa   i.
               (Please give me one sheet of paper.)

7. ___ ___ ___ ___ ___ ん ___ ___ 、 ___ ___ ___ ___ ___。
   Ya   ma   mo   to   se   n   se   i   sa   yo   o   na   ra.
               (Mr./Ms. Yamamoto, good-bye.)

Start from the right column. s = stop, t = tail, h = hook.　　　　　　　　↓

N		O (Particle)		WA
ん		を		わ
ん		を		わ
ん		を		わ

27　　　　　　　　　　　　　　　　　　　　　ひらがな

【 よみましょう : Let's read.】

1.	かわ	river
2.	わし	eagle
3.	わに	crocodile; alligator
4.	にわ	garden, yard
5.	まんが	comic
6.	みかん	tangarine

7.	せんそう	war
8.	べんとう	box lunch
9.	てんぷら	tempura
10.	わんわん	bow wow
11.	なっとう	fermented soy bean
12.	てっぽう	gun

【 かきましょう : Let's write.】

I. Fill in the blanks with the correct *hiragana*. Use は for the topic particle WA.

1. ＿＿＿ ＿＿＿ ＿＿＿ ＿＿＿ ＿＿＿ ＿＿＿ ＿＿＿ ＿＿＿ ＿＿＿。 (I am Honda.)
   Wa　　ta　　shi　　wa (P)　　Ho　　n　　da　　de　　su.

2. ＿＿＿ ＿＿＿ ＿＿＿ ＿＿＿ ＿＿＿ ＿＿＿ ＿＿＿ ＿＿＿。 (What is that?)
   So　　re　　wa (P)　　na　　n　　de　　su　　ka.

(Is this yours?)

3. ＿＿ ＿＿ ＿＿ ＿＿ ＿＿ ＿＿ ＿＿、＿＿ ＿＿ ＿＿ ＿＿ ＿＿。
   Ya　ma　da　se　n　se　i　　ko　n　ni　chi　wa.(P)
   (Mr./Ms. Yamada, hello.)

4. ＿＿ ＿＿ ＿＿ ＿＿ ＿＿ ＿＿ ＿＿ ＿＿ ＿＿ ＿＿ ＿＿。
   Yu　k　ku　ri　o　ne　ga　i　shi　ma　su.
   (Slowly, please.)

5. ＿＿ ＿＿ ＿＿ ＿＿ ＿＿ ＿＿。 (I do not understand.)
   Wa　ka　ri　ma　se　n.

6. ＿＿ ＿＿ ＿＿ ＿＿ ＿＿ ＿＿ ＿＿ ＿＿。 (Please give me an exam.)
   Shi　ke　n　o (P)　ku　da　sa　i.

7. ＿＿ ＿＿ ＿＿ ＿＿ ＿＿ ＿＿ ＿＿ ＿＿。 (Please sit down.)
   Su　wa　t　te　ku　da　sa　i.

8. ＿＿ ＿＿ ＿＿ ＿＿ (pencil)　　9. ＿＿ ＿＿ (book)
   e　n　pi　tsu　　　　　　　　ho　n

なまえ：_____

ひづけ：_____

The small や, ゆ, and よ are used only with the *hiragana* in the -I rows of *hiragana*. That is, they are used after *hiragana* きぎしじちにひびぴみり.

The position of small ゃゅょ. Ex. きゃ

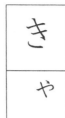

1. きゃ **KYA**   きゅ **KYU**   きょ **KYO**

2. ぎゃ **GYA**   ぎゅ **GYU**   ぎょ **GYO**

3. しゃ **SHA**   しゅ **SHU**   しょ **SHO**

4. じゃ **JA**   じゅ **JU**   じょ **JO**

5. ちゃ **CHA**   ちゅ **CHU**   ちょ **CHO**

6. にゃ **NYA**   にゅ **NYU**   にょ **NYO**

7. ひゃ **HYA**   ひゅ **HYU**   ひょ **HYO**

8. びゃ **BYA**   びゅ **BYU**   びょ **BYO**

9. ぴゃ **PYA**   ぴゅ **PYU**   ぴょ **PYO**

10. みゃ **MYA**   みゅ **MYU**   みょ **MYO**

11. りゃ **RYA**   りゅ **RYU**   りょ **RYO**

ひらがな

ひらがな１１-２（きゃ〜りょ）　　　なまえ：_____

【 よみましょう : Let's read.】

1. りょこう　　　travel
2. しゃしん　　　photo
3. びょういん　　hospital
4. きゅうり　　　cucumber
5. ぎゅうにゅう　(cow) milk

6. りゅう　　　　dragon
7. にんぎょう　　doll
8. ちょうちょう　butterfly
9. じゅぎょう　　class instruction
10. じゃんけんぽん　*jan-ken-pon*

【 かきましょう : Let's write.】

I. Fill in the blanks with the correct *hiragana*.

1. _____ _____ _____ _____ _____ _____ _____ 。(Let's begin.)
　　Ha　　ji　　me　　ma　　sho　　　o.

2. _____ _____ 　_____ _____ _____ _____ 。(190)
　　Hya　　ku　　　kyu　　u　　ju　　u.

3. _____ _____ _____ _____ 。(Sit down.)
　　Cha　　ku　　se　　ki.

4. _____ _____ _____ _____ _____ (text)　5. _____ _____ _____ (dictionary)
　　kyo　　o　　ka　　sho　　　　　　　ji　　sho

6. _____ _____ _____ _____ (homework)　7. _____ _____ _____ テスト (quiz)
　　shu　　ku　　da　　i　　　　　　　sho　　o　　te su to

8. _____ _____ _____ _____ (photo)　9. _____ _____ _____ _____ _____ (China)
　　sha　　shi　　n　　　　　　　chu　　u　　go　　ku

10. _____ _____ _____ _____ _____ _____ _____ _____ _____ (7th grade)
　　chu　　u　　ga　　ku　　i　　chi　　ne　　n　　se　　i

11. _____ _____ _____ _____ _____ (doctor)　12. _____ _____ _____ (housewife)
　　o　　i　　sha　　sa　　n　　　　　　shu　　fu

13. _____ _____ _____ _____ _____ (hospital)
　　byo　　o　　i　　n

ORIGINS OF HIRAGANA: PART 4

	Hiragana	Kaisho	Gyoosho	Soosho
MA	ま	末	末	ま
MI	み	美	美	み
MU	む	武	武	む
ME	め	女	女	め
MO	も	毛	毛	も

	Hiragana	Kaisho	Gyoosho	Soosho
YA	や	也	也	や
YU	ゆ	由	由	ゆ
YO	よ	与	与	与

	Hiragana	Kaisho	Gyoosho	Soosho
RA	ら	良	良	ら
RI	り	利	利	り
RU	る	留	留	る
RE	れ	禮	禮	れ
RO	ろ	呂	呂	ろ

	Hiragana	Kaisho	Gyoosho	Soosho
WA	わ	和	和	わ
O	を	遠	遠	を
N	ん	无	无	ん

ひらがな

カタカナ

なまえ: _____

ひづけ: _____

Start from the right column. s = stop, t = tail, h = hook. ↓

お	え	う	い	あ
オ	エ	ウ	イ	ア
オ	エ	ウ	イ	ア
オ	エ	ウ	イ	ア

カタカナ

アドベンチャー日本語1

カタカナ１－２

A. Vertically

Start here.
↓

(Long vowel)			wo		we		wi		ye
	l		ウ		ウ		ウ		イ
			オ		エ		イ		エ
			ウ		ウ		ウ		イ
			オ		エ		イ		エ

B. Horizontally

→

ye	イ	エ	イ	エ			
wi	ウ	イ	ウ	イ			
we	ウ	エ	ウ	エ			
wo	ウ	オ	ウ	オ			
(Long vowel)	ー	-----					

カタカナ

34

アドベンチャー日本語1
カタカナ1－3   なまえ：＿＿＿＿＿＿＿＿＿＿＿＿＿＿＿
（アイウエオ／イェ／ウィ／ウェ／ウォ／ー） ひづけ：＿＿＿＿＿＿＿＿＿＿＿＿＿＿

I. Write the *hiragana* equivalents.

1. オ （　） 　 2. ウ （　） 　 3. エ （　） 　 4. ア （　） 　 5. イ （　）

II. The following *katakana* are Chinese last names. Match them with those in the box below.

1. ウーさん （　）　　 2. イーさん （　）　　 3. アウさん （　）

A. Mr. Au   B. Mr. Wu   C. Mr. Yee

III. Choose the *katakana* combinations from the box below which would be used in writing the initial
sound of the following words.

1. week （　）　　　　 2. walk （　）　　　　 3. Wendy （　）　　　　 4. whiskey （　）

5. water （　）　　　 6. (Mr.) Yates （　）　 7. wedding （　）　　　 8. waiter （　）

A. イェ　　 B. ウィ　　 C. ウェ　　 D. ウォ

IV. Write the correct *katakana* in the (　). Use ア／イ／ウ／エ／オ／イェ／ウィ／ウェ／ウォ／ー.
Use ー for long vowel sounds. The small *katakana* occupies its own space.

1. ice　　　　　　（　　）（　　）（　ス　）
　　　　　　　　　　　a　　　　i　　　　su

2. auto　　　　　（　　）（　　）（　ト　）
　　　　　　　　　　o　　　　o　　　　to

3. eight　　　　　（　　）（　　）（　ト　）
　　　　　　　　　　e　　　　i　　　　to

4. week　　　　　（　　）（　）（　　）（　ク　）
　　　　　　　　　　wi　　　　i　　　　ku

5. walkman　　　（　　）（　）（　　）（　ク　）（　マ　）（　ン　）
　　　　　　　　　　wo　　　　o　　　　ku　　　ma　　　n

6. waiter　　　　（　　）（　）（　　）（　タ　）（　　）
　　　　　　　　　　we　　　　i　　　　ta　　　　a

カタカナ

にほんのまんが

なまえ: _____

ひづけ: _____

Start from the right column. s = stop, t = tail, h = hook.　　　　　　　↓

こ	け	く	き	か
コ	ケ	ク	キ	カ
	コ ケ	ケ ク	キ	カ
	コ ケ	ケ ク	キ	カ

カタカナ

なまえ: _____

ひづけ: _____

Start from the right column. s = stop, t = tail, h = hook.　　　　　　↓

ご	げ	ぐ	ぎ	が
ゴ	ゲ	グ	ギ	ガ
ゴ	ゲ	グ	ギ	ガ
ゴ	ゲ	グ	ギ	ガ

なまえ:＿＿＿＿＿＿＿＿＿＿＿＿

A. Vertically

Start here.
↓

		gwa			kwo			kwa
		グ			ク			ク
		ア			オ			ア
		グ			ク			ク
		ア			オ			ア

B. Horizontally

Start here.
→

kwa ク	ア	ク	ア				
kwo ク	オ	ク	オ				
gwa グ	ア	グ	ア				

カタカナ

カタカナ２−４

（カ キ ク ケ オ／ガ ギ グ ゲ ゴ／クァ／クォ／グァ）

I. Write the *hiragana* equivalents.

　　1. ゲ（　）　　2. ク（　）　　3. ケ（　）　　4. ア（　）　　5. ギ（　）

　　6. カ（　）　　7. ウ（　）　　8. エ（　）　　9. オ（　）　　10. キ（　）

　　11. コ（　）　12. グ（　）　13. ゴ（　）　14. ガ（　）　15. イ（　）

II. These are Japanese first names. Find the same names in *hiragana* in the box. Circle the one name which belongs to a male.

　　1. アキオ（　）　　2. アイコ（　）　　3. エイコ（　）　　4. ケイコ（　）

　　| A.あいこ　　B.あきお　　C.けいこ　　D.えいこ |

III. These are Japanese last names. Match them with the same names in *hiragana* .

　　1. アオキ（　）　　2. コイケ（　）　　3. アカイ（　）　　4. アカイケ（　）

　　5. アカオ（　）　　6. ウエキ（　）　　7. オウエ（　）　　8. イゲ　　　（　）

　　| A.うえき　　　B.あかい　　C.あおき　　　D.あかお |
　　| E.あかいけ　　F.こいけ　　G.いげ　　　　H.おうえ |

IV. Choose the *katakana* combinations from the box below which would be used to write the underlined portions of the following words.

　　1. winter（　）　　2. guava（　）　　　3. waitress（　）　　4. walk（　）

　　5. quarter（　）　6. Yeltsin（　）　　7. iguana（　）

　　| A.イェ　　B.ウィ　　C.ウェ　　D.ウォ　　E.クァ　　F.クォ　　G.グァ |

V. Complete the following words by writing the correct *katakana* in the parentheses.

1. milk [MIRUKU]　ミ ル（MI RU　　）　　6. U.S. [AMERIKA]（　　）メ リ（ME RI　）

2. video [BIDEO]　ビ デ（BI DE　　）　　7. garage [GAREEJI]（　　）レ（RE　）ジ（JI）

3. toilet [TOIRE]　ト（TO　）レ（RE）　　8. coffee [KOOHII]（　　）（　　）ヒ（HI　）（　）

4. piano [PIANO]　ピ（PI　）ノ（NO）　　9. cafeteria [KAFETERIA]

5. guitar [GITAA]　（　）タ（TA　）　　　　　　　（　　）フェ テ リ（FE TE RI　）

なまえ:＿＿＿＿＿＿＿＿＿＿＿＿＿＿

ひづけ:＿＿＿＿＿＿＿＿＿＿＿＿＿＿

Start from the right column. s = stop, t = tail, h = hook.   ↓

そ	せ	す	し	さ
ソ	セ	ス	シ	サ
ソ	セ	ス	シ	サ
ソ	セ	ス	シ	サ

カタカナ

なまえ: ＿＿＿＿＿＿＿＿＿＿＿＿＿

ひづけ: ＿＿＿＿＿＿＿＿＿＿＿＿＿

Start from the right column. s = stop, t = tail, h = hook.   ↓

ぞ		ぜ		ず		じ		ざ	
	ゾ		ゼ		ズ		ジ		ザ
	ゾ		ゼ		ズ		ジ		ザ

なまえ: _____

A. Vertically

Start here.
↓

		je			she
		ジ			シ
		エ			エ
		ジ			シ
		エ			エ

B. Horizontally

Start here.
→

she	シ	エ	シ	エ				
je	ジ	エ	ジ	エ				

43

カタカナ

I. Write the *hiragana* equivalents.

    1. グ（ ）   2. ズ（ ）   3. ケ（ ）   4. シ（ ）   5. ギ（ ）

    6. ゾ（ ）   7. サ（ ）   8. エ（ ）   9. ア（ ）   10. ス（ ）

    11. コ（ ）   12. ソ（ ）   13. ジ（ ）   14. セ（ ）   15. ゼ（ ）

II. Match the *hiragana* and *katakana* readings of the following Japanese last names.

    1. アサイ　（ ） 2. アサオ（ ）   3. アカイ（ ）   4. サカウエ　（ ）

    5. オオサカ（ ） 6. イシイ（ ）   7. キシ　（ ）   8. スガ　　　（ ）

    9. ソウガ　（ ）10. セガ　（ ）   11. アソウ（ ） 12. ウジイエ　（ ）

A.おおさか	B.あかい	C.うじいえ	D.すが
E.きし	F.あさい	G.せが	H.そうが
I. いしい	J.さかうえ	K.あさお	L.あそう

III. Onomatopoetic Expressions: Match the onomatopoetic expressions from the box with the pictures below.

    1. （　　）

    2. （　　）

    3. （　　）

    4. （　　）

    5. （　　）

A. キー！
B. エイ！
C. イー！
D. グーグー
E. ザーザー

IV. Complete the following words by writing the correct *katakana* in the parentheses.

1. garage [GAREEJI]   (   ) レ^{RE} (   ) (   )

2. Spain [SUPEIN]   (   ) ペ^{PE} (   ) ン^N

3. radio [RAJIO]   ラ^{RA} (   ) (   )

4. orange [ORENJI]   (   ) レ ン^{RE N} (   )

5. taxi [TAKUSHII]   タ^{TA} (   ) (   ) (   )

6. waitress [WEITORESU]   (   ) (   ) (   ) ト レ^{TO RE} (   )

7. ice [AISU]   (   ) (   ) (   )

V. Identify the *katakana* combinations from the box below which would be used to write the underlined portions of the following words.

1. Jane   (   )   2. guava (   )   3. waitress (   )   4. wink   (   )

5. quarter (   )   6. Yale (   )   7. Water   (   )   8. shake (   )

A. イェ	B. ウィ	C. ウェ	D. ウォ
E. クォ	F. グァ	G. シェ	H. ジェ

45   カタカナ

どこですか？

A. アフリカ
B. アメリカ
C. サウスアメリカ
D. オーストラリア
E. スペイン
F. メキシコ
G. フランス

パリ
（　　）

マドリッド
（　　）

（　　）

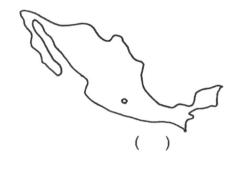

（　　）

（　　）

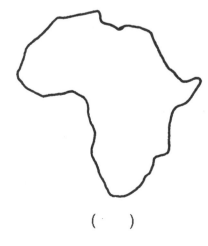

（　　）

（　　）

カタカナ

46

なまえ: _____

ひづけ: _____

Start from the right column. s = stop, t = tail, h = hook.　　　　　　　　↓

と	て	つ ＊	ち	た
ト	テ	ツ	チ	タ
	ト	テ	ツ	チ	タ
	ト	テ	ツ	チ	タ

＊ **Compare: シ (shi) and ツ (tsu)**

47

なまえ: _____

ひづけ: _____

Start from the right column. s = stop, t = tail, h = hook.　　　　　　　　↓

ど	で	（づ）＊	ぢ ＊	だ
ド	デ	ツ	ヂ	ダ
ド	デ	ツ	ヂ	ダ

＊ These *katakana* are rarely used.

なまえ: _____

A. Vertically

Start here.
↓

	di		ti		tso		tse		tsa		che
	デ		テ		ツ		ツ		ツ		チ
	イ		イ		オ		エ		ア		エ
	デ		テ		ツ		ツ		ツ		チ
	イ		イ		オ		エ		ア		エ

B. Horizontally

Start here.
→

che	チ	エ	チ	エ							
tsa	ツ	ア	ツ	ア							
tse	ツ	エ	ツ	エ							
tso	ツ	オ	ツ	オ							
ti	テ	イ	テ	イ							
di	デ	イ	デ	イ							

カタカナ

I. Write the *hiragana* equivalents.

    1. テ（   ） 2. ゾ（   ） 3. ケ（   ） 4. タ（   ） 5. シ（   ）

    6. ド（   ） 7. ウ（   ） 8. ト（   ） 9. オ（   ） 10. デ（   ）

    11. ズ（   ） 12. グ（   ） 13. チ（   ） 14. サ（   ） 15. ツ（   ）

II. Match the *katakana* and *hiragana* readings of the following Japanese last names.

    1. アキタ（ ）   2. アシダ（ ）   3. タオカ（ ）   4. ウエダ   （ ）

    5. オカダ（ ）   6. オキタ（ ）   7. タケダ（ ）   8. サカタ   （ ）

    9. イシダ（ ）   10. ダテ   （ ）   11. ドイ   （ ）   12. タキシタ （ ）

A. おかだ	B. たおか	C. いしだ	D. さかた
E. あしだ	F. うえだ	G. だて	H. たけだ
I. あきた	J. おきた	K. どい	L. たきした

III. Match the *katakana* names with their English equivalents.

    1. スー（ ）   2. スージー（ ）   3. ジェシカ（ ） 4. ケーシー（ ）

    5. ダック or ドック（ ）   6. アート   （ ） 7. ジェシー（ ）

    8. タッド or トッド（ ）   9. ディック（ ） 10. ティー   （ ）

A. Doc	B. Todd	C. Suzie	D. Art
E. Jessica	F. Sue	G. Jessie	H. Tee
I. Dick	J. Casey		

IV. Read the following *katakana* words. Then write their English equivalents. Use the hints in brackets.

	English		English
1. チェ リー [fruit]	_____	5. フォ ーク [utensil]	_____
2. ディック [name]	_____	6. ディ ナー [meal]	_____
3. アイスティー [drink]	_____	7. ティー シャ ツ [clothing]	_____
4. キャ ンディー [sweet]	_____	8. チェス [game]	_____

V. Onomatopoetic Expressions: Match the onomatopoetic expressions with the correct pictures.

1. (　　)  　　2. (　　)  　　3. (　　)

 4. (　　)

A. ドキドキ
B. シー
C. コケコッコー
D. カッカ

VI. Complete the following words.

1. video [BIDEO] 　　　　　　ビ (　BI　) (　　　)

2. Spain [SUPEIN] 　　　　　(　　) ペ (　N　) ン　（PE）

3. chocolate [CHOKOREETO] チョ (　CHO　) レ (　RE　) (　　)

4. Canada [KANADA] 　　　　(　　) ナ (　NA　)

5. taxi [TAKUSHII] 　　　　　(　　) (　　) (　　) (　　)

6. Germany [DOITSU] 　　　　(　　) (　　) (　　)

7. computer [KONPYUUTAA] (　N　) ンピュ (　PYU　) (　　) (　　)

8. toilet [TOIRE] 　　　　　　(　　) (　　) レ　（RE）

9. guitar [GITAA] 　　　　　　(　　) (　　) (　　)

51

カタカナ

なんのスポーツですか？

(　　)　　　　　(　　)　　　　　(　　)　　　　　(　　)

A.	テニス
B.	スイミング
C.	スキー
D.	ジョギング
E.	ゴルフ
F.	サッカー
G.	フットボール
H.	バスケットボール
I.	ベースボール
J.	バレーボール
K.	ランニング

(　　)　　　　　　　　　　　　　　　　　　　(　　)

(　　)　　　　　　　　　　　　　　　　　　　(　　)

(　　)　　　　　(　　)　　　　　(　　)

なまえ: _____

ひづけ: _____

Start from the right column. s = stop, t = tail, h = hook.   ↓

の	ね	ぬ	に	な
ノ	衤	又	二	ナ
ノ	衤	ヌ	二	ナ
ノ	衤	ヌ	二	ナ

カタカナ

I. Write the *hiragana* equivalents.

1. ニ（　　）2. ツ（　　）3. ネ（　　）4. テ（　　）5. ヌ（　　）
6. ス（　　）7. ケ（　　）8. ウ（　　）9. ノ（　　）10. サ（　　）
11. タ（　　）12. ナ（　　）13. ト（　　）14. オ（　　）15. チ（　　）
16. イ（　　）17. ア（　　）18. エ（　　）19. ソ（　　）20. キ（　　）
21. ク（　　）22. カ（　　）23. シ（　　）24. コ（　　）25. セ（　　）

II. Match the *katakana* names with their English equivalents.

1. ジーナ　（　）2. ジェニー（　）3. ジニー　（　）4. ケニー　（　）
5. トニー　（　）6. ダニー　（　）7. シドニー（　）8. ネッド　（　）

| A. Kenny | B. Ginny | C. Gina | D. Danny |
| E. Jenny | F. Sydney | G. Ned | H. Tony |

III. Write the English equivalents of the *katakana* words below. Use the cues given in the brackets.

English

1. カヌー [sport]　　＿＿＿＿＿＿

2. ソニー [company]　＿＿＿＿＿＿

3. ディナー [meal]　　＿＿＿＿＿＿

4. ノート [stationery]　＿＿＿＿＿＿

5. スキー [sport]　　＿＿＿＿＿＿

6. スケート [sport]　＿＿＿＿＿＿

English

7. スノーケル [sport]　＿＿＿＿＿＿

8. カップヌードル [food]　＿＿＿＿＿＿

9. スノーボード [sport]　＿＿＿＿＿＿

10. スナックバー [place]　＿＿＿＿＿＿

11. セイコー [company]　＿＿＿＿＿＿

12. テニス [sport]　　＿＿＿＿＿＿

IV. Onomatopoetic Expressions: Circle the expression which matches the drawing.

A. ゲラゲラ

B. ワッハッハ

C. オッホホ

D. ニコニコ

なまえ: _____

ひづけ: _____

Start from the right column. s = stop, t = tail, h = hook.   ↓

ほ		へ		ふ		ひ		は	
求		へ		フ		ヒ		ハ	
	ホ		へ		フ		ヒ		ハ
	ホ		へ		フ		ヒ		ハ

カタカナ

なまえ: _____

ひづけ: _____

Start from the right column. s = stop, t = tail, h = hook. ↓

ぼ	べ	ぶ	び	ば
ポ	ベ	ブ	ビ	バ
ポ	ベ	ブ	ビ	バ
ポ	ベ	ブ	ビ	バ

なまえ: _____

ひづけ: _____

Start from the right column. s = stop, t = tail, h = hook. ↓

ぽ	ぺ	ぷ	ぴ	ぱ
ポ	ペ	プ	ピ	パ
ポ	ペ	プ	ピ	パ
ポ	ペ	プ	ピ	パ

カタカナ 6－4

A. Vertically

Start here.
↓

	fo		fe		fi		fa
	フ		フ		フ		フ
	オ		エ		イ		ア
	フ		フ		フ		フ
	オ		エ		イ		ア

B. Horizontally

Start here.
→

fa	フ	ァ	フ	ァ			
fi	フ	ィ	フ	ィ			
fe	フ	ェ	フ	ェ			
fo	フ	ォ	フ	ォ			

アドベンチャー日本語1

なまえ：＿＿＿＿＿＿＿＿＿＿＿＿＿＿＿

カタカナ6－5

ひづけ：＿＿＿＿＿＿＿＿＿＿＿＿＿＿＿

（ハヒフヘホ／バビブベボ／パピプペポ／ファフィフェフォ）

I. Write the *hiragana* equivalents.

　　1. ヒ（　　） 　2. チ（　　） 　3. ツ（　　） 　4. バ（　　） 　5. ヘ（　　）
　　6. ブ（　　） 　7. ノ（　　） 　8. ビ（　　） 　9. テ（　　） 　10. ポ（　　）
　　11. ホ（　　） 　12. ハ（　　） 　13. シ（　　） 　14. ペ（　　） 　15. フ（　　）
　　16. ヌ（　　） 　17. ト（　　） 　18. サ（　　） 　19. ソ（　　） 　20. ネ（　　）
　　21. ナ（　　） 　22. ニ（　　） 　23. オ（　　） 　24. ス（　　） 　25. タ（　　）

II. Match the *katakana* readings with the English names.

　　1. ハイジ　（　　） 　　2. ボブ（　　） 　　3. ピーター（　　） 　　4. フランク（　　）
　　5. ベッキー（　　） 　　6. ベン（　　） 　　7. ポール　（　　） 　　8. ポーラ　（　　）

A. Bob	B. Frank	C. Paula	D. Becky
E. Ben	F. Heidi	G. Paul	H. Peter

III. Write the English equivalents. Use the cues given in brackets.

English

1. ポップコーン [food] ＿＿＿＿＿＿＿

2. フォーク [utensil] ＿＿＿＿＿＿＿

3. カフェテリア [place] ＿＿＿＿＿＿＿

4. フィッシング [sport] ＿＿＿＿＿＿＿

5. フォト [thing] ＿＿＿＿＿＿＿

6. フェンシング [sport] ＿＿＿＿＿＿＿

English

7. ボールペン [thing] ＿＿＿＿＿＿＿

8. ピーナッツ [food] ＿＿＿＿＿＿＿

9. フィンランド [country] ＿＿＿＿＿＿＿

10. ドーナツ [food] ＿＿＿＿＿＿＿

11. ピンポン [sport] ＿＿＿＿＿＿＿

12. フィラデルフィア [city] ＿＿＿＿＿＿＿

カタカナ

IV. Onomatopoetic Expressions: Match expressions with pictures.

1. (   )

2. (   )

3. (   )

4. (   )
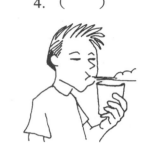

5. (   )

6. (   )

eat one after the other

A. パチパチ　　B. ピーピー　　C. フーフー

D. パクパク　　E. ブーブー　　F. ピカピカ

V. Write the following words in *katakana*.

1. piano [PIANO]　　　　（　　）（　　）（　　）

2. coffee [KOOHII]　　　（　　）（　　）（　　）（　　）

3. video [BIDEO]　　　　（　　）（　　）（　　）

4. Spain [SUPEIN]　　　（　　）（　　）（　　）　ン

5. cafeteria [KAFETERIA]（　　）（　　）（　　）（　　）リ（　　）

6. picnic [PIKUNIKKU]　（　　）（　　）（　　）（　）（　　）

7. pink [PINKU]　　　　（　　）ン（　　）

8. golf [GORUFU]　　　（　　）ル（　　）

9. party [PAATII]　　　（　　）（　　）（　　）（　）（　　）

10. sports [SUPOOTSU]　（　　）（　　）（　　）（　　）

カタカナ

60

なまえ: _____

ひづけ: _____

Start from the right column. s = stop, t = tail, h = hook.   ↓

も		め		む		み		ま	
	モ		メ		ム		ミ		マ
	モ		メ		ム		ミ		マ
	モ		メ		ム		ミ		マ

I. Write the *hiragana* equivalents.

1. ヌ （　　） 2. ミ （　　） 3. ゾ （　　） 4. メ （　　） 5. ビ （　　）
6. バ （　　） 7. チ （　　） 8. ノ （　　） 9. ス （　　） 10. ツ （　　）
11. テ （　　） 12. プ （　　） 13. マ （　　） 14. セ （　　） 15. モ （　　）
16. ム （　　） 17. ク （　　） 18. エ （　　） 19. タ （　　） 20. シ （　　）
21. ゴ （　　） 22. ネ （　　） 23. ト （　　） 24. ポ （　　） 25. ナ （　　）

II. Match the *katakana* names with their English equivalents.

1. マリー　（　　） 2. ミリー　（　　） 3. タミー　（　　） 4. キム　（　　）
5. ティム　（　　） 6. マドンナ（　　） 7. トム　（　　） 8. ジミー（　　）
9. メリー　（　　） 10. マイク　（　　） 11. ミッキー（　　） 12. エミー（　　）
13. エミリー（　　） 14. ジム　（　　） 15. モリス　（　　） 16. マック（　　）

A. Kim	B. Tom	C. Tim	D. Jimmy
E. Marie	F. Emily	G. Amy	H. Morris
I. Tammy	J. Jim	K. Millie	L. Mike
M. Mac	N. Mary	O. Madonna	P. Mickey

III. Write the English equivalents.　Use the hints given in brackets.

English

1. ハム [food] _____
2. ガム [snack] _____
3. ホットドッグ [food] _____
4. ハンバーガー [food] _____
5. ピザ [food] _____
6. スパゲッティ [food] _____
7. パンケーキ [food] _____

English

8. ミルク [drink] _____
9. ビール [drink] _____
10. ペプシコーラ [drink] _____
11. マクドナルド [place] _____
12. アイスクリーム [food] _____
13. モーツァルト [composer] _____
14. ストロベリー [food] _____

なまえ: _____

IV. Onomatopoetic Expressions: Match the expressions with the appropriate pictures.

1. (　　)    2. (　　)    3. (　　)

4. (　　)

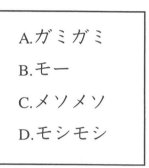

> A. ガミガミ
> B. モー
> C. メソメソ
> D. モシモシ

V. Write the *katakana* equivalents of the following words.

1. U.S. [AMERIKA]   (　　) (　　) リ (　　)

2. milk [MIRUKU]   (　　) ル (　　)

3. walkman [WOOKUMAN]   (　　) (　　) (　　) (　　) (　　) ン

カタカナ

なんのベジタブル？　なんのフルーツ？

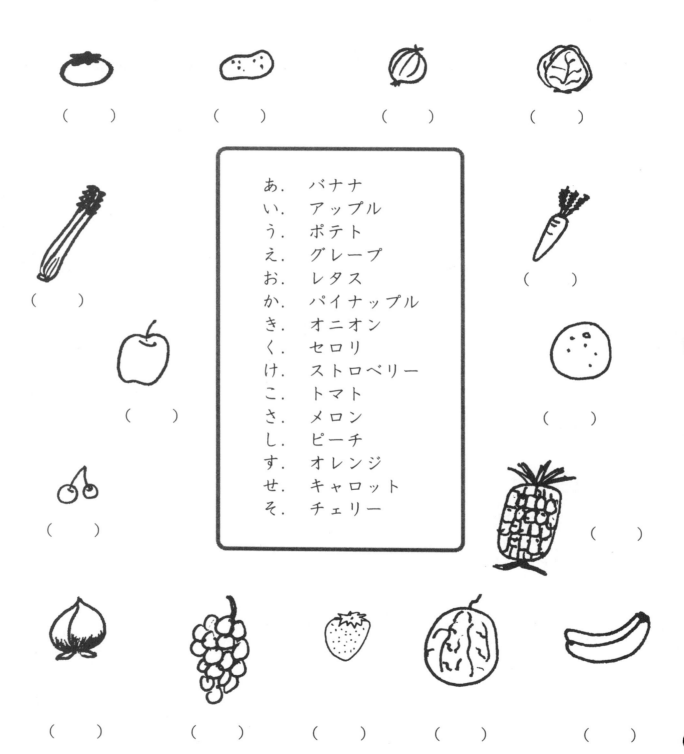

( )　　　( )　　　( )　　　( )

あ．バナナ
い．アップル
う．ポテト
え．グレープ
お．レタス
か．パイナップル
き．オニオン
く．セロリ
け．ストロベリー
こ．トマト
さ．メロン
し．ピーチ
す．オレンジ
せ．キャロット
そ．チェリー

( )　　　( )

( )　　　( )

( )　　　( )

( )　　　( )　　　( )　　　( )　　　( )

なまえ: _____

ひづけ: _____

Start from the right column. s = stop, t = tail, h = hook.　　　　　　　　↓

	よ			ゆ			や
	ヨ			ユ			ヤ
	ヨ			ユ			ヤ
	ヨ			ユ			ヤ

カタカナ

Start here.
↓

A. Vertically

hyo	hyu	hya	nyo	nyu	nya	cho	chu	cha	sho	shu	sha	kyo	kyu	kya
ヒ	ヒ	ヒ	ニ	ニ	ニ	チ	チ	チ	シ	シ	シ	キ	キ	キ
ヨ	ユ	ヤ	ヨ	ユ	ヤ	ヨ	ユ	ヤ	ヨ	ユ	ヤ	ヨ	ユ	ヤ
ヒ	ヒ	ヒ	ニ	ニ	ニ	チ	チ	チ	シ	シ	シ	キ	キ	キ
ヨ	ユ	ヤ	ヨ	ユ	ヤ	ヨ	ユ	ヤ	ヨ	ユ	ヤ	ヨ	ユ	ヤ

↓

pyo	pyu	pya	byo	byu	bya	jo	ju	ja	gyo	gyu	gya	myo	myu	mya
ピ	ピ	ピ	ビ	ビ	ビ	ジ	ジ	ジ	ギ	ギ	ギ	ミ	ミ	ミ
ヨ	ユ	ヤ	ヨ	ユ	ヤ	ヨ	ユ	ヤ	ヨ	ユ	ヤ	ヨ	ユ	ヤ
ピ	ピ	ピ	ビ	ビ	ビ	ジ	ジ	ジ	ギ	ギ	ギ	ミ	ミ	ミ
ヨ	ユ	ヤ	ヨ	ユ	ヤ	ヨ	ユ	ヤ	ヨ	ユ	ヤ	ヨ	ユ	ヤ

なまえ: _____

B. Horizontally

Start here.

→

kya	キ	ャ				
kyu	キ	ュ				
kyo	キ	ョ				
sha	シ	ャ				
shu	シ	ュ				
sho	シ	ョ				
cha	チ	ャ				
chu	チ	ュ				
cho	チ	ョ				
nya	ニ	ャ				
nyu	ニ	ュ				
nyo	ニ	ョ				
hya	ヒ	ャ				
hyu	ヒ	ュ				
hyo	ヒ	ョ				

→

mya	ミ	ャ				
myu	ミ	ュ				
myo	ミ	ョ				
gya	ギ	ャ				
gyu	ギ	ュ				
gyo	ギ	ョ				
ja	ジ	ャ				
ju	ジ	ュ				
jo	ジ	ョ				
bya	ビ	ャ				
byu	ビ	ュ				
byo	ビ	ョ				
pya	ピ	ャ				
pyu	ピ	ュ				
pyo	ピ	ョ				

67

カタカナ

アドベンチャー日本語1　　　　　　　　なまえ:＿＿＿＿＿＿＿＿＿＿＿＿

カタカナ8－4

（ヤユヨ／キャ～ピョ）

I. Write the *hiragana* equivalents.

1. ム（　　） 2. ニ（　　　） 3. モ（　　） 4. フ（　　） 5. ヤ（　　）

6. ヌ（　　） 7. ノ（　　　） 8. マ（　　） 9. ナ（　　） 10. チ（　　）

11. ホ（　　） 12. ヒ（　　） 13. シ（　　） 14. ユ（　　） 15. ソ（　　）

16. ミ（　　） 17. テ（　　） 18. ト（　　） 19. ネ（　　） 20. ヘ（　　）

21. ツ（　　） 22. メ（　　） 23. ヨ（　　） 24. ハ（　　） 25. タ（　　）

II. Match the *katakana* names with their English equivalents.

1. ジョイ　　　（　） 2. ジョージ（　） 3. ジャッキー（　） 4. ジュリー　（　）

5. ジュディー（　） 6. ショーン（　） 7. ジェフ　　（　） 8. ジョン　　（　）

9. ギャビン　（　） 10. ケシャ　（　） 11. ミッシェル（　） 12. ジェシカ（　）

13. ユーニス　（　） 14. キャシー（　） 15. チャーリー（　） 16. ジョシュア（　）

A. Gavin	B. Jackie	C. Eunice	D. Cathy
E. Jon	F. Judy	G. Julie	H. Charlie
I. Joy	J. Jeff	K. Sean	L. Joshua
M. Jessica	N. Kesha	O. Michelle	P. George

III. Here are some baseball terms in *katakana*. Guess what they are in English.

　　　　　　　　English　　　　　　　　　　　　　　　　　　　　　　English

1. ベースボール＿＿＿＿＿＿　　　　　9. ボール　　　　＿＿＿＿＿＿

2. キャッチャー＿＿＿＿＿＿　　　　　10. ファウル　　　＿＿＿＿＿＿

3. ピッチャー　＿＿＿＿＿＿　　　　　11. アウト　　　　＿＿＿＿＿＿

4. コーチ　　　＿＿＿＿＿＿　　　　　12. セーフ　　　　＿＿＿＿＿＿

5. マネージャー＿＿＿＿＿＿　　　　　13. スチール　　　＿＿＿＿＿＿

6. バット　　　＿＿＿＿＿＿　　　　　14. ホームラン　　＿＿＿＿＿＿

7. グローブ　　＿＿＿＿＿＿　　　　　15. アンパイヤー　＿＿＿＿＿＿

8. ストライク　＿＿＿＿＿＿　　　　　16. スコアー　　　＿＿＿＿＿＿

IV. Onomatopoetic Expressions: Match the expressions with the appropriate picture.

1. (　　)

2. (　　)

3. (　　)

4. (　　)

5. (　　)

6. (　　)

7. (　　)

A. キャー ！
B. チューチュー
C. チュッ
D. メチャクチャ
E. ヤッター！
F. オギャーオギャー
G. ペチャクチャ

V. Write the following words in *katakana*.

1. computer [KONPYUUTAA]　　(　　) ン (　　) (　) (　　) (　　) (　　)

2. chocolate [CHOKOREETO]　　(　　) (　) (　　) レ (　　) (　　)

3. jogging [JOGINGU]　　(　　) (　) (　　) ン (　　)

4. juice [JUUSU]　　(　　) (　) (　　) (　　)

カタカナ

なんですか？

( )    ( )   ( ) 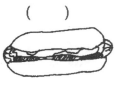   ( )

 ( )

あ．	ホットドッグ
い．	ミルク
う．	ジュース
え．	サンドイッチ
お．	ナイフ
か．	ピザ
き．	フォーク
く．	フライドポテト
け．	コーラ
こ．	スプーン
さ．	コップ
し．	コーヒー
す．	ハンバーガー
せ．	チョコレート
そ．	ナプキン
た．	ストロー

( )

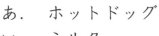

( )

 ( )

( )

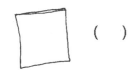 ( )

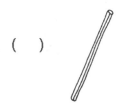 ( )

( )

 ( )    ( )    ( )    ( )

なまえ: _____

ひづけ: _____

Start from the right column. s = stop, t = tail, h = hook. ↓

ろ	れ	る	り	ら
口	レ	ル	リ	ラ
口	レ	ル	リ	ラ
口	レ	ル	リ	ラ

カタカナ

Start here.
↓

A. Vertically

		ryo			ryu			rya
		リ			リ			リ
		ヨ			ユ			ヤ
		リ			リ			リ
		ヨ			ユ			ヤ

B. Horizontally

Start here.
→

rya	リ	ヤ	リ	ヤ							
ryu	リ	ユ	リ	ユ							
ryo	リ	ヨ	リ	ヨ							

I. Write the *hiragana* equivalents.

1.ハ（　　） 2.レ（　　） 3.モ（　　） 4.ヤ（　　） 5.ロ（　　）

6.ヨ（　　） 7.ム（　　） 8.ネ（　　） 9.ホ（　　） 10.ノ（　　）

11.フ（　　） 12.マ（　　） 13.ラ（　　） 14.ツ（　　） 15.ユ（　　）

16.ナ（　　） 17.ヌ（　　） 18.ス（　　） 19.リ（　　） 20.チ（　　）

21.ル（　　） 22.ヒ（　　） 23.メ（　　） 24.ト（　　） 25.ミ（　　）

26.オ（　　） 27.ク（　　） 28.ウ（　　） 29.コ（　　） 30.ア（　　）

II. Match the *katakana* names with their English equivalents.

1.キャラ（　） 2.レスリー（　） 3.ウィリー（　） 4.アレン（　）

5.ドーラ（　） 6.ローリー（　） 7.ケリー（　） 8.テリー（　）

9.ノラ（　） 10.リッキー（　） 11.サリー（　） 12.レイチェル（　）

13.ハリー（　） 14.ネリー（　） 15.クリス（　） 16.マリー（　）

17.リック（　） 18.ライアン（　） 19.ビル（　） 20.アンディー（　）

A. Nora	B. Nellie	C. Rick	D. Rachel
E. Alan	F. Dora	G. Marie	H. Ricky
I. Cara	J. Harry	K. Sally	L. Bill
M. Andy	N. Chris	O. Leslie	P. Terry
Q. Ryan	R. Lori	S. Kelie	T. Willy

III. Many computer terms are written in *katakana*. Guess what these are in English.

English

1.プリンター ＿＿＿＿＿

2.スクリーン ＿＿＿＿＿

3.イーメール ＿＿＿＿＿

4.マウス ＿＿＿＿＿

5.アップル ＿＿＿＿＿

English

6.マニュアル ＿＿＿＿＿

7.プログラム ＿＿＿＿＿

8.ファイル ＿＿＿＿＿

9.グラフィック ＿＿＿＿＿

10.ダブルクリック ＿＿＿＿＿

カタカナ

IV. Onomatopoetic Expressions: Match the expressions with the appropriate pictures.

1. (　　)

2. (　　)

3. (　　)

crazy!

4. (　　)

A. コラッ！

B. ガッカリ

C. ボロボロ

D. クルクルパー

V. Write the following words in *katakana*.

1. U.S. [AMERIKA] (　　) (　　) (　　) (　　)

2. radio [RAJIO] (　　) (　　) (　　)

3. chocolate [CHOKOREETO] (　　) (　) (　　) (　　) (　　) (　　)

4. milk [MIRUKU] (　　) (　　) (　　)

5. cola [KOORA] (　　) (　　) (　　)

6. cafeteria [KAFETERIA] (　　) (　　) (　) (　　) (　　) (　　)

7. toilet [TOIRE] (　　) (　　) (　　)

8. locker [ROKKAA] (　　) (　) (　　) (　　)

9. ballpoint pen [BOORUPEN] (　　) (　　) (　　) (　　) ン

10. orange [ORENJI] (　　) (　　) ン (　　)

11. T.V. [TEREBI] (　　) (　　) (　　)

12. golf [GORUFU] (　　) (　　) (　　)

なまえ:＿＿＿＿＿＿＿＿＿＿＿＿＿＿＿＿

ひづけ:＿＿＿＿＿＿＿＿＿＿＿＿＿＿＿＿

Start from the right column. s = stop, t = tail, h = hook.　　　　　　　　　↓

ん		を		わ

Compare: ソ "SO" and ン "N", ワ "WA" and ク "KU"

75

カタカナ

I. Write the *hiragana* equivalents.

1. ン （　） 　2. ソ （　） 　3. シ （　） 　4. ツ （　） 　5. タ （　）
6. ク （　） 　7. ネ （　） 　8. ワ （　） 　9. ウ （　） 　10. コ （　）
11. ユ （　） 　12. テ （　） 　13. ノ （　） 　14. メ （　） 　15. ナ （　）
16. フ （　） 　17. ラ （　） 　18. マ （　） 　19. ム （　） 　20. ヤ （　）
21. セ （　） 　22. ロ （　） 　23. ヨ （　） 　24. レ （　） 　25. ル （　）
26. ア （　） 　27. オ （　） 　28. イ （　） 　29. ケ （　） 　30. サ （　）

II. Match the *katakana* names with their English equivalents.

1. ジョン （　） 　2. リン （　） 　3. リンダ （　） 　4. マリアン （　）
5. ベン （　） 　6. ジョアン （　） 　7. ジェイン （　） 　8. リリアン （　）
9. ケン （　） 　10. イレイン （　） 　11. ダン （　） 　12. キャレン （　）
13. アン （　） 　14. ダイアン （　） 　15. ヘレン （　） 　16. ダレン （　）

A. Ken	B. Darren	C. Lynn	D. Ben
E. Diane	F. John	G. Elaine	H. Karen
I. Ann	J. Dan	K. Lillian	L. Marian
M. Helen	N. JoAnn	O. Jane	P. Linda

III. Many sports related words are written in *katakana*. Guess what these sports are in English.

	English		English
1. レスリング	_____	6. マラソン	_____
2. ピンポン	_____	7. ダイビング	_____
3. ソフトボール	_____	8. サーフィン	_____
4. アイスホッケー	_____	9. スイミング	_____
5. ジョギング	_____	10. サッカー	_____

なまえ:＿＿＿＿＿＿＿＿＿＿＿＿＿＿

IV. Onomatopoetic Expressions: Match the expressions with the appropriate pictures.

1. (　　)　　　　　　　2. (　　)　　　　　　　3. (　　)

4. (　　)　　　　　　　5. (　　)　　　　　　　6. (　　)

　　sneezing　　　　　　　　coughing

A.ハクション	D.ワンワン
B.ニャーンニャーン	E.プンプン
C.ワッハッハ	F.ゴホンゴホン

V. Complete the following words in *katakana*.

1. France [FURANSU]　　　　(　　) (　　) (　　) (　　)

2. Spain [SUPEIN]　　　　　(　　) (　　) (　　) (　　)

3. walkman [WOOKUMAN]　　(　　) (　) (　　) (　　) (　　) (　　)

4. computer [KONPYUUTAA]　(　　) (　　) (　　) (　) (　　) (　　) (　　)

5. pink [PINKU]　　　　　　(　) (　　) (　　)

6. orange [ORENJI]　　　　　(　) (　　) (　　) (　　)

7. dance [DANSU]　　　　　(　　) (　　) (　　)

　　　　　　　　　　カタカナ

なまえ: _____

ひづけ: _____

Start here.
↓

I. A. Vertically

	vyu		vo		ve		vi		va
	ヴ		ヴ		ヴ		ヴ		ヴ
	ユ		オ		エ		イ		ア
	ヴ		ヴ		ヴ		ヴ		ヴ
	ユ		オ		エ		イ		ア

B. Horizontally

Start here.
→

va	ヴ	ァ	ヴ	ァ					
vi	ヴ	ィ	ヴ	ィ					
ve	ヴ	ェ	ヴ	ェ					
vo	ヴ	ォ	ヴ	ォ					
vyu	ヴ	ュ	ヴ	ュ					

II. What are these musical instruments?

1. ヴァイオリン _____

2. ヴィオラ _____

Kana Flashcards

ひらがなフラッシュカード

ひらがなフラッシュカード

83

ひらがなフラッシュカード

ひらがなフラッシュカード

87

ひらがなフラッシュカード

あ あたま かくして しり かくさず

え えんは いなもの あじなもの

き きいて ごくらく みて じごく

い いぬも あるけば ぼうに あたる

お おいては こに したがい

く くさいものに ふたを する

う うそから でた まこと

か かわいいこには たびをさせ

け けがの こうみょう

Hide your head, but you can't hide your buttocks.

[Even if you hide one bad thing, you cannot hide another.]

Fate is a mysterious and meaningful thing.

[Strange and romantic is the affinity that binds people in relationships.]

Hearing is paradise; seeing is hell.

[Hearing about something and seeing it are completely different.]

Even dogs will run into sticks/rods.

[If you meddle, you will encounter trouble.]
[A flying crow always catches something.]

Old folks, follow your children.

[When one gets old, it is better to listen to what your children say.]

Cover smelly things.

[Hiding bad things as though they do not exist.]
["Hush up" things.]

Truth emerges from lies.

[Although one may have planned to say it as a lie, it turned out to be the truth.]

Allow your beloved child to travel.

[In order to encourage your child to see the world in its broadest sense, you must educate your child and allow them to experience the world.]

An achievement by mistake.

[To win by a fluke.]

た び は みちづれ よ は なさけ	す きこそ ものの じょうずなり	こ は さんがいの くびっかせ
ち りも つもれば やまと なる	せ に はらは かえられぬ	さ んべん まわって たばこに しよう
つ きよに かまを とぐ	そ うりょうの じんろく	し らぬが ほとけ

ひらがなフラッシュカード

Children are a burden
through our three
incarnations (past,
present, futute).
[Parents will sacrifice to
any extent for the sake of
their children.]
[Parents are forever encum-
bered by their children.]

Because you enjoy it,
you become even more
skilled at it.

[Preferences show
where one's talent lies.]

In travelling,
companionship; in life,
kindness/sympathy.
[In travelling,
companionship is
important, but in life,
we should help out one
another through
cooperation.]

Turn three times, then
have a cigarette.

[Do your job, then rest.]

The back and stomach
cannot be interchanged.

[For the sake of the
most cherished sacrifice
something cherished less.]

Even rubbish, when
accumulated, becomes
a mountain.

[Even something
insignificant will become
big when it collects.]

Not knowing is
(like) Buddha.

[As long as you don't
know about something,
it will not bother you.]
[Where ignorance is
bliss, 'tis folly to be
wise.]

The eldest child is
a simpleton.

[First born, least clever.]
[The first born are more
docile than their siblings.]

Sharpen your sickle in
the moonlight.
(Be prepared for the
next day.)

[Carelessness will result
in failure.]
[Don't be caught off
guard.]

の どもと すぎれば あつさを わすれる	に くまれっこ よに はばかる	て いしゅの すきな あかえぼし
は なより だんご	ぬ すびとの ひるね	と しよりの ひやみず
ひ ょうたんから こまが でる	ね んには ねんを いれ	な きっつらに はち

The headgear which the master likes. [The family follows the preferences of its master.] [Husband's taste becomes his wife's.]	A troubled child will be frowned upon by the rest of the world. [Ill weeds grow apace (are sure to thrive).] [Weeds never die.]	Once it passes through your throat, you will forget how hot it was. [When danger passes, God is forgotten.] [Once on shore, we pray no more.]
An old man's cold water. (Cold water is inappropriate for an old man.) [Indiscretion of an old man.] [An old man not knowing how to be prudent.]	A burglar's nap. (A burglar naps during the day, is re-energized for the night.) [One must prepare well to successfully commit an act.]	Dumplings rather than cherry blossoms. [Bread is better than the song of birds.]
Being stung on a crying face. [Misfortune piles up yet again on misfortune.] [One misfortune rides upon another's back.] [Misfortunes seldom come alone.]	Be careful with your precaution. [It is never enough to be careful.] [One can never be careful enough.]	A horse emerges from a gourd. [Unexpected things appear from unexpected places.]

ふ ろしきを ひろげる

ま けるが かち

め うえの たんこぶ

へ たな よこずき

み から でた さび

も んぜんの こぞう ならわぬ きょうを よむ

ほ ねおりぞんの くたびれ もうけ

む りが とおれば どうりが ひっこむ

や すものかいの ぜに うしない

ひらがなフラッシュカード

Spread out a *furoshiki*. [To say things in an exaggerated way.] [Talking big.]	Losing is winning. [Giving a victory to your competitor is a victory for you.] [Stoop to conquer.]	A bump above one's eye. [A thorn in one's side.] [Pain in the neck.]
Unskillful, but likes it. [Although unskillful at it, he enjoys it.]	Rust emerged from the flesh. [One suffers for one's mistakes.]	A boy in front of a temple will chant the sutra untaught. [One will learn effort- lessly if one is in the environment.]
Even if one breaks his bones, he only becomes exhausted and ineffective. [Gained nothing despite all the efforts.]	If unreasonableness is acceptable, justice withdraws. [Where might is master, justice is servant.]	Buy cheap things and waste your money. [Cheap things are of poor quality and in the long run, you will lose more.]

ゆだん たいてき

りょうやくは
くちに にがし

ろんより
しょうこ

よしのずいから
てんじょう
のぞく

るりも はりも
みがけば ひかる

われなべに
とじぶた

らく あれば
く ある

れいせつを
しる

おぼれるものは
わらをも
つかむ

Carelessness is a foe. [One will fail if one is not careful.]	Good medicine is bitter to the taste. [Honest advice is hard to accept.]	Evidence rather than theory. [Make decisions on proof rather than on conjecture.] [Proof is better than argument.]
Looking at the skies through the stem of a reed. [Looking at the large world from a small place.]	Where you polish a gem or a needle, it will shine. [As long as you work at it, you will become great (rewarded).]	A mended lid for a cracked pot. [Bad things draw together.]
After pleasure, comes suffering. [Things are never always rosy.]	Know proper decorum. [It is important to be courteous.]	A drowning man will reach for even a straw. [When in desperation, we will grab on to anything, no matter how small.]

ス	ケ	オ	ア
セ	コ	カ	イ
ソ	サ	キ	ウ
タ	シ	ク	エ

99

カタカナフラッシュカード

ヘ	ノ	ナ	チ
ホ	ハ	ニ	ツ
マ	ヒ	ヌ	テ
ミ	フ	ネ	ト

カタカナフラッシュカード

ヲ	ル	ユ	ム
ン	レ	ヨ	メ
	ロ	ラ	モ
	ワ	リ	ヤ

カタカナフラッシュカード